THE WORLD ACCORDING TO
TRUMP

THE WORLD ACCORDING TO
TRUMP

AN UNAUTHORIZED PORTRAIT
IN HIS OWN WORDS

KEN LAWRENCE

**Andrews McMeel
Publishing**

Kansas City

05 06 07 08 09 RR2 10 9 8 7 6 5 4 3 2 1

ISBN: 0-7407-5012-7

Library of Congress Control Number: 2004111410

Book design and composition by
Kelly & Company, Lee's Summit, Missouri

ATTENTION: SCHOOLS AND BUSINESSES

Andrews McMeel books are available at quantity discounts with bulk purchase for educational, business, or sales promotional use. For information, please write to: Special Sales Department, Andrews McMeel Publishing, 4520 Main Street, Kansas City, Missouri 64111.

Contents

Introduction

The Trump name has become synonymous with tall buildings, casinos, glitz, glamour, and even a top-rated reality TV show. The man with the funny-looking hair and the signature line "You're fired!" has captured our imagination like few other businesspeople of our generation.

Donald John Trump was born June 14, 1946, in New York. His father, Fred, was a deal maker and real estate entrepreneur who focused on properties in Queens and Brooklyn after World War II, building affordable apartments for the middle class and profiting handsomely.

Donald went a different route. After graduating from a military academy, he attended the prestigious University of Pennsylvania's Wharton School where he studied finance. After graduation, he worked with his father, then set out to make his own mark in real estate. His target was Manhattan, where real estate prices were much higher.

By the 1980s, Trump had had many triumphs, including Trump Tower on Fifth Avenue, Trump Parc, and the Plaza Hotel. He also bought casinos in Atlantic City. The key to his success was not just finding the right property but negotiating the right deal and selling properties at the right time. For a while, it seemed as if he had the Midas touch, and his properties commanded high rents and attracted prominent clients.

Trump was also a tireless promoter, placing his name in large letters on many of his buildings and on the aircraft of the Trump Shuttle, a small commuter airline he bought from American Airlines and later sold. He wrote a book about his experiences titled *Trump: The Art of the Deal* (1988), which became a best seller, and in 1990 he followed it with *Trump: Surviving at the Top,* another best seller.

By the mid-1990s, however, the strong real estate market in New York had weakened, and Trump's leveraged properties were put under pressure. His empire seemed to crumble overnight as banks forced him into business bankruptcy because he could not pay over $2 billon in loans. He barely escaped personal bankruptcy. He sold some properties to meet payments and skillfully negotiated payouts to creditors as well as tax breaks and other considerations from the city. By focusing on what he did best—deal making—Trump was able to pull himself out of debt and once again become New York's golden boy of real estate.

In 1997, he wrote another best seller about his rise from the ashes titled *Trump: The Art of the Comeback.* He expanded his empire to golf courses and beauty pageants, partnering with NBC in the Miss Universe, Miss USA, and Miss Teen USA Pageants.

He even made a short-lived effort at running for president on the Reform Party ticket in 1990. Trump insisted that his political intentions were honest, but his detractors claimed it was a publicity stunt to bring the Trump name into the public consciousness. Being president would not have worked for Trump, anyway. A self-admitted germophobe, he does not shake hands with strangers, calling it a "barbaric custom."

For all his business success, however, his personal life suffered. Trump divorced Ivana, his wife of thirteen years, in a 1990 settlement marred by charges of womanizing. It was Ivana who nicknamed him "The Donald." The couple has three children, including Ivanka, a rising young model. In 1993, Trump married model Marla Maples, but they divorced six years later. They have one daughter, Tiffany. Currently, Trump is engaged to international model Melania Knauss, a thirty-three-year-old native of Slovenia.

In 2003, Trump partnered with Mark Burnett, creator of the hit TV show *Survivor,* on *The Apprentice.* The show features Trump and staff members judging contestants on how well they run various business ventures. A monster smash hit, the show raised Trump to national cult status. Again, he took advantage of his popularity with a best-selling book, *Trump: How to Get Rich.*

Here, then, is Donald Trump, in his own words.

On *The Apprentice*

It's funny; I always thought I was a
celebrity, but when you have a smash
television show, there is something
very big about that. What is funny,
a friend of mine said, "All you do
(on the show) is fire people and
yet—you're shown to have much
more heart than people thought
you had." It's actually softened
my image—that's a little strange.

Los Angeles Daily News
MARCH 29, 2004

It's *Survivor,* but it's the real survivor.
It's in the jungle of New York.

> *Larry King Live*
> APRIL 18, 2004

*In this interview, Trump claimed to be
the highest-paid person in prime-time
television:*

More than Oprah? "Oprah's not
prime time."

More than Larry King? "Yeah, and
Larry King is cable."

More than the *Friends* cast? "Well,
collectively, no," he acknowledged.
"But individually, yes."

> *New York Times*
> MARCH 28, 2004

On "You're fired!":

There's a beauty in those two words. When you utter those words, there's very little that can be said. There's a succinctness to those words.

San Francisco Chronicle
MARCH 28, 2004

[The contestants] have tremendous IQs. Some are close to 200, which is the upper, upper part of the scale. I am amazed at what they have been able to do. But in a few cases, I've been amazed at their total stupidity.

Deseret (Utah) Morning News
MARCH 25, 2004

Now, all of a sudden, I have a *Variety* on my desk, where I never did before. All of a sudden, I'm looking at ratings whereas, six months ago, I didn't know what a rating was.

Philadelphia Inquirer
MARCH 20, 2004

Trump was hoping to copyright the phrase "You're fired!":

Every time you walk down the street people are screaming, "You're fired!" It's in case I ever decide to do something with it.

New York Post
MARCH 19, 2004

All the networks bid on it, everybody wanted it. We went with NBC because they run the Miss Universe contest.

Copley News Service
APRIL 25, 2004

When contestant Bill Rancic won the apprentice spot, he was given two choices: manage a Trump-owned golf course in California or oversee a ninety-story building project in Chicago:

In a way, I'm very happy he didn't choose the golf course, 'cause I put someone there about a month and a half ago, and they're doing a great job.

Deseret (Utah) Morning News
APRIL 17, 2004

At some point, I have to go on with my life. I'm not going to be on the show forever. Hopefully someone will replace me who's going to carry the show on to—I can't say great heights, but to the same heights or even slightly less, and that would be satisfactory.

> *Centre Daily Times*
> (State College, Pennsylvania)
> APRIL 15, 2004

I'm glad that NBC is trying something radically different: a new show that isn't a spin-off of *Law & Order.*

> Associated Press
> NOVEMBER 25, 2003

I loved [this show] because it highlighted New York and it highlighted
business. It was a smart show
involving smart people—not the
dummies I see on some of these
other shows.

Contra Costa Times
(Walnut Creek, California)
APRIL 15, 2004

What surprised me most was how
easily the women dominated
initially. Yet when the women were
put with the men, they lost their
dominance. I don't know why.
Maybe that's a reflection of real life.

Houston Chronicle
APRIL 8, 2004

I hated it when one of the contestants said she'd never been duped before in her life. I'm a smart guy and I get duped all the time.

Copley News Service
APRIL 25, 2004

That's the only part of the show that's a little bit unrealistic. I've terminated many people, but I seldom use those two words, unless someone does something very egregious, like stealing. I wouldn't want to use those words to a good person who tried to do the job but just couldn't do it. That would be brutal.

San Francisco Chronicle
MARCH 28, 2004

*Trump laments that the show allows
people to learn more about his behavior
and that may give potential competitors
an edge in business dealings:*

My life is like a game of poker.
And they see you and they see
you dealing with these people and
they'll figure out your mind and
they'll try to figure out your steps.
People will be able to figure me out
more easily.

Pittsburgh Post-Gazette
APRIL 11, 2004

On Business

People say, "Do you have the same opportunity today as you had years ago?" And I say, "Absolutely." You always have an opportunity. There's always an opportunity, especially in this country.

CNN's *Late Edition with Wolf Blitzer*
MARCH 21, 2004

Words are cheap, results are what it's all about.

New York Post
MARCH 19, 2004

I'd much rather have a really smart, talented guy doing a deal in a not-so-good location than an idiot doing a deal at a great location.

Associated Press
JANUARY 7, 2004

I don't like firing people. It's not a pleasant thing and it's sad. . . . In some cases, it's a terrible, terrible situation for the person who gets fired, how strongly they take it. So it's not something that any rational or sane person can love doing, but it also happens to be a fact of life in business.

Boston Herald
JANUARY 7, 2004

I used to think it wasn't possible to
be overaggressive. But some of the
contestants [on *The Apprentice*] have
shown me that, in fact, you can be
too aggressive for the situation.

Saint Paul Pioneer Press
APRIL 15, 2004

It's wonderful to believe in the
power of positive thinking and
all, but they're all after your job.
They're all after your position.
They're all after your money.
I've never seen a great businessman
who wasn't a little bit paranoid.

USA Today
MARCH 12, 2004

Never beg when you're trying to sell
something. If it doesn't work out,
take your lumps and relax.

> *Chicago Tribune*
> MARCH 11, 2004

We agree it's much better to solve
certain issues outside the courtroom
than inside.

> *Press Journal*
> (Vero Beach, Florida)
> FEBRUARY 15, 1998

I believe in being paid on the back
end and getting a lot if it sells a lot.
I believe in compensation for success,
not just gouging some company up
front.

> *Deseret (Utah) Morning News*
> JANUARY 30, 2004

We hunt for pleasure. So you have to really be a little bit paranoid. There are so many stories about people who have been decimated by people they trusted.

> *Hoya* (Georgetown University)
> DECEMBER 4, 2001

The stock market is very scary. Put [your money] in some good, strong interest-bearing accounts. I'm very concerned about the stock market.

> *Seattle Post-Intelligencer*
> SEPTEMBER 4, 1998

I think promotion is a wonderful thing; it sells product.

> *USA Today*
> FEBRUARY 6, 2004

I've had a lot of luck over the years
with women executives and this
[Trump's beauty pageants] is something that cried out for women
executives.

Associated Press
AUGUST 14, 1998

I understand one thing. There is a
difference between a man buying
for business and buying personally.
I have seen people who will kill in
business for an extra nickel and yet
will spend $5 million for a great
apartment the next day. They just
want the best.

Financial Times
JUNE 15, 1996

When you're doing business, you take people to the brink of breaking them without having them break, to the maximum point their head can handle. . . . That's the sign of a good businessman.

Playboy
MARCH 1990

You have to surround yourself with people that are going to tell you—look, number one, smart people have ideas. You're smart. They're smart. And you take a lot of ideas, and then you have to make a decision. But you have to surround yourself with people that are going to push ideas.

The Oprah Winfrey Show
APRIL 8, 2004

I think in business [compared to politics] in a certain way—and this is going to sound a little strange—you're probably a little bit more honest, if you want to know the truth.

Capital Report
JANUARY 29, 2004

You lose a lot of the economy if interest rates start drifting up, and they are starting. You have to keep interest rates low so the economy, real estate, and other aspects of the economy continues strong.

Your World with Neil Cavuto
DECEMBER 15, 2003

I think the regulations are very tough, but I think they could be made tougher. And where they really have to be made tougher is when somebody is proven to be dishonest, not a mistake, not an honest mistake because look, people make bad business deals all the time. When somebody is proven to be dishonest, really harsh punishment has to take place.

Hardball with Chris Matthews
JULY 15, 2002

I can tell right away if a guy is a winner or a loser just by the way he conducts himself on the course.

Golf Magazine
NOVEMBER 1993

People may not always think big themselves, but they can still get very excited by those who do. That's why a little hyperbole never hurts.

> *Los Angeles Times,*
> citing *The Art of the Deal*
> FEBRUARY 14, 1994

I was turning over too much of my business to guys like that. I figured, Why should I do everything? Let those guys handle it. But you have to have touch.

> *Playboy*
> MAY 1997

I have featured and will always continue to feature my name prominently in all my enterprises.

> *Business Week*
> JULY 22, 1985

Trump is sometimes compared to real estate developer William Zeckendorf, who was responsible for the United Nations, Century City in Los Angeles, and Place Ville Marie in Montreal. Zeckendorf eventually went bankrupt:

I used him as a model in a sense. He was a great visionary but he wasn't fiscally conservative. Having seen the way he went down taught me to be overly so.

New York Times
AUGUST 7, 1983

I like to hire people that I've seen in action. I often hire people that were on the opposing side of a deal that I respect.

Washington Post
SEPTEMBER 23, 1989

On Casinos and Gambling

I love Atlantic City. It's been good
to me, and I've been good to it.
I've been there a long time, and
I have no plans of leaving.

Philadelphia Inquirer
APRIL 5, 2004

Everybody had this perception of
Gary [Indiana] as not being the
greatest place in the world. It was
certainly a challenge. We built an
incredible oasis.

Associated Press
MARCH 4, 1999

I love building beautiful apartment houses, but I'd make a lot more money building a beautiful casino.

San Jose Mercury News
SEPTEMBER 6, 2000

Trump's show The Apprentice *has been good for the share price of Trump Hotels, which had hit a low of $1.51 in 2003:*

If anything, the brand has gotten more valuable because of the show. I think the name has helped the casinos in terms of the drawing of the crowds.

New York Times
MARCH 28, 2004

In 1993, Trump fought the idea of Indian-owned casinos in New York State. Although he said it was because casinos would be detrimental to people in the area, others believe he did not want competition for his casinos in Atlantic City. Trump later had to defend himself against charges of racism and bigotry for his comments:

They don't look like Indians to me and they don't look like Indians to Indians. . . . It will be the biggest scandal since Al Capone and it will destroy the gambling industry. . . . It's obvious that organized crime is rampant on the Indian reservations.

> Senate hearing in
> Washington, D.C.
> MAY 1993

Steve Wynn claimed that two former employees of his Mirage resort passed on trade secrets to Trump in an effort to attract high rollers from Asia to Trump's Taj Mahal in Atlantic City:

I don't have to use such tricks to attract the high rollers. I've got 'em already. That's why Wynn is so desperate to get into Atlantic City— it's where the action is.

> *New York Post*
> APRIL 22, 1999

Well, I've always liked Las Vegas. I think it's a terrific place. But they have overbuilt.

> CNBC's *Business Center*
> JULY 14, 1999

Gaming is a very double-edged sword. It both giveth and taketh away in terms of an economy.

Honolulu Star-Bulletin
MAY 8, 1998

Perhaps it wouldn't be so bad if there was no gaming in the United States, but if it's not gaming, it's horses. If it's not horses, it's something else. Or it's, excuse me, it's the stock market because that's the biggest casino in the world when you get right down to it anyway.

Evans & Novak
DECEMBER 27, 1997

I have glitzy casinos because people expect it. I'm not going to build the lobby of the IBM building in Trump Castle.

Playboy
MARCH 1990

Trump opposed Quick Draw, a lottery-type, real-time, monitored, government-run game proposed for New York. Proponents of the game said Trump was concerned about competition from the government for betting dollars:

This will be a total disaster for the social and economic fabric of New York. This will destroy families. They're going to be putting all their money into a video crack game, which is all it is.

New York Daily News
SEPTEMBER 2, 1995

More about Quick Draw:

People won't be paying rent.
They won't be buying cars, food,
or clothing. The big problem will be
that your welfare rolls will go up.
There may be some overflow with
my casinos, but the big loser will be
the state.

> *New York Times*
> AUGUST 23, 1995

*Speaking about an aerial circus
proposed for the Taj Mahal:*

We're going to have to have nets,
but you know, it would be more
exciting if you had that little extra
element of thrill, of not knowing if
one of the trapeze guys was going
to go splat!

> *New York Times*
> JULY 26, 1996

For the most part, 95 percent, 96
percent, [of gamblers] go there for
recreation. They love it. . . . They
have friends. They go down with
a limited amount of money. It's
that 4 percent or 5 percent that
is a problem. There's no question
about it.

Hardball with Chris Matthews
NOVEMBER 19, 1999

*Trump bought Adnan Khashoggi's
282-foot yacht for $30 million:*

While I was building this marina
[in Atlantic City], I was trying to
get the boat, because I knew that
it would blow everybody's mind.

Toronto Star
AUGUST 7, 1988

The overwhelming number of people who go to casinos do so for limited periods of time with set budgets. Almost all of the people who gamble at Atlantic City or Las Vegas must take a bus, plane, or long car ride to get there.

National Law Journal
SEPTEMBER 4, 1995

At the Tyson-Holmes fight in January, the pit drop at our two casinos, Trump Plaza and Trump Castle, was $15 million more than it would have been without the fight.

New York Times
MAY 1, 1988

Everyone said stay away from
Atlantic City. Everybody but about
four guys [heeded the warning].
I was one of the four.

> *New York Times*
> APRIL 8, 1984

*Trump spent hundreds of millions
of dollars renovating and rebuilding
casinos and hotels in Atlantic City:*

In ten years, as I look back, I'm going
to say I'm glad I invested the money.
Short-term I wish I didn't do it.

> *Fortune*
> AUGUST 13, 1990

About the Taj Mahal:

It's truly going to be an incredible place. We're calling it the eighth wonder of the world. I think it's going to do huge numbers. The overall majesty of the building is what's going to attract people. People are just amazed at the opulence.

> *Washington Post*
> MARCH 25, 1990

Again, the Taj Mahal:

It's a billion-dollar hotel, and it looks it.

> *Time*
> APRIL 9, 1990

After trying to demolish the home of a long-time Atlantic City resident to make way for a parking lot for limousines, Trump appeared bitter:

Did she put on her old clothing for you? The bottom line is, it's too bad for Atlantic City, but it's not too bad for me because I'm not interested in the property. Nobody gets under my skin.

New York Daily News
JULY 26, 1998

I've never gambled in my life. To me, a gambler is someone who plays slot machines. I prefer to own slot machines. It's a very good business being the house.

Time
APRIL 9, 1990

On Deals and Deal Making

There's a beauty to making a great deal. It's my canvas and I like painting it.

Playboy
MARCH 1990

It's exciting, and part of the reason it's exciting is because they're mega-deals, they're important deals, they're glamorous deals. Everybody talks about them, everybody reads about them and writes about them. There's a level of importance there that I think also somewhat turns me on.

Saturday Night With Connie Chung
FEBRUARY 24, 1990

Sometimes, winners are difficult people, but I'd rather work with someone difficult.

New York Daily News
SEPTEMBER 26, 1995

I'm a real estate person. Some people are newspaper guys. But I'm a real estate guy. I'm always looking for the next deal.

Times (London)
JUNE 19, 1996

Well, I think that the celebrity probably helps my deals. I didn't really start out wanting to be a celebrity—it just sort of happened.

CTV News
JULY 14, 2001

I said, "I will build you this incredible, gorgeous, gleaming hotel. I will put people to work in the construction trades and save hotel jobs and the Grand Central area will come around." So the city made the deal.

New York Times
AUGUST 7, 1983

About the $400 million he paid for the Plaza hotel:

To me, that's the best [deal] of all.

New York Times
DECEMBER 27, 1988

I look at things for the art sake and the beauty sake and for the deal sake.

Toronto Star
AUGUST 7, 1988

*On setting the record-breaking $1,500
price for ringside seats at the Mike
Tyson–Michael Spinks world heavy-
weight title fight in Atlantic City:*

I wanted to go to $2,000. If we had,
we would've sold the same number
of tickets by the exact same time. But
when we set the prices, Don King and
my Trump Plaza executives, Steve
Hyde and Mark Etess, convinced me
that $1,500 was the right number.
I still think we would've gotten the
$2,000, but enough is enough.

New York Times
MAY 1, 1988

People think of Trump as being
difficult to work with. I'm not . . .
except with people I don't respect.

Business Week
JULY 20, 1987

Upon completing a deal with Merv Griffin in which Trump got the unfinished Taj Mahal casino and Griffin got the rest of Resorts International:

He paid me a fortune and I got the crown jewel. Beating Merv was a lot of fun.

New York Times
DECEMBER 27, 1988

Trump negotiated for fifteen months with the city of New Rochelle for rights to develop Davids Island. The price was $13 million but Trump offered $12,999,999.99:

Being superstitious, I thought I might make it a little bit complicated.

New York Daily News
JANUARY 12, 1996

I said to the bankers, "Listen, fellows, if I have a problem, then you have a problem. We have to find a way out or it's going to be a difficult time for both of us."

> *Fortune*
> AUGUST 13, 1990

I'm not big on compromise. I understand compromise. Sometimes compromise is the right answer, but oftentimes compromise is the equivalent of defeat, and I don't like being defeated.

> *Life*
> JANUARY 1989

Some people have an ability to negotiate. It's an art you're basically born with. You either have it or you don't.

> *Washington Post*
> NOVEMBER 15, 1984

On Family

I did want to prove to my father and other people that I had the ability to be successful on my own.

Playboy
MARCH 1990

I think I was a good husband in many respects, but I think I was a bad husband when it came to devoting time.

The Geraldo Rivera Show
MAY 16, 1997

Not many sons have been able to escape their fathers.

New York Times
AUGUST 7, 1983

The part of my life I think I'm most disappointed in is that I have not had the great marriage. And I would have thought that would have happened, because I came from a home—you know, it's not like some of my friends, they get divorced, but their parents were divorced twice or three times. I came from a home where marriage was just incredible. I mean, my parents truly loved each other.

Good Morning America
DECEMBER 2, 1999

I believe in the institution of marriage. There's nothing better. It beats being the world's greatest playboy by a million, but sometimes you don't have a choice.

Hardball with Chris Matthews
NOVEMBER 19, 1999

On Friends and Acquaintances

My life is all business. People I deal
with in business become my friends.

Buffalo News
APRIL 14, 2004

If you help somebody and they don't
help you, you know, this has created
disloyalty, and I don't like disloyal
people. I'm a very loyal person.

USA Today
NOVEMBER 3, 1997

George [Steinbrenner] is one of the city's most underappreciated assets. He's a good friend of mine and he will do right for all of New York. George has the puzzle figured out long before the game is being played. That's what I love about him.

New York Daily News
SEPTEMBER 26, 1995

On Jack Welch, former CEO of General Electric:

He's probably the greatest corporate leader in history.

CNN.com
NOVEMBER 29, 1999

On Martha Stewart:

Well, Martha's a friend of mine, so I have a little bit of a prejudice in that sense. I know her. She's a good woman. She gets terrible press; she gets an unfair press. She's certainly a tough woman. You know, if Martha were a man, they'd say, "Oh, what a great businessperson. What a tough person," and they'd say it glowingly. But as a woman, there's a double standard. They say she's a—you know, they use the B-word. And the fact is, it's not true. She's a very fine woman, I've known her for a long time, and I think she'll be fine.

Capital Report
JANUARY 29, 2004

On Jesse Ventura:

Well, I think he's a terrific guy.
I think he's very smart. He speaks
plainly and the truth and boom.
And I just think that Jesse has made
an impact on the country.

> *Rivera Live*
> NOVEMBER 26, 1999

On Golf

A guest at Trump's International Golf Club in West Palm Beach killed a fifty-pound black swan that had been given to Trump as a gift. The man said it was in self-defense:

I spoke with the member and relayed to him that his guest is not to set foot on any of my properties again. I don't care if it was self-defense or not. The actions seemed excessive.

Chicago Sun-Times
JANUARY 18, 2001

I think golf is more of a bonding
thing. I don't know what it is. You
can take people out to lunch and at
the end of the lunch you have no
idea who they are, but at the end of
a round of golf, you're best friends.

USA Today
MARCH 1, 2000

I like shaping land. I get a real
thrill from buying it and shaping
it beautifully and artistically. It's a
whole other thing from building
a ninety-story tower across from
the U.N.

New York Times
MAY 28, 2000

*Trump is a member of the Winged Foot
Golf Club, which is so exclusive it
reportedly has a fifteen-year waiting
list. Trump was asked if former President
Clinton could ever become a member:*

It wouldn't have been tough for him
to get in, but for the scandals. . . .
He's not going to get in.

Orlando Sentinel
JANUARY 9, 2000

But Trump had an offer:

I'm building a beautiful golf club
five minutes from his home, and
I would be happy to have him as
a member.

Orlando Sentinel
JANUARY 9, 2000

*In buying trees for one of his golf clubs,
Trump was amazed at finding a bargain
in royal palms usually costing up to
$5,000 for only $300 each:*

Somebody once sent me flowers—
roses. The roses were $300. How
could a tree that grows fifty feet
up in the air cost only $300?

> *Palm Beach Post*
> JANUARY 5, 2000

Well, I no longer feel guilty about
playing golf because now I can say
I do it for, you know, work, so it
works out pretty well.

> *Wall $treet Week with Fortune*
> JULY 26, 2002

When Trump opened Club Mar-a-Lago, one member wanted his $25,000 membership fee returned because he said he was promised that celebrities would be around for him to mingle with, and two that attended on opening day—Tony Bennett and Lee Majors—were not high-caliber enough for him:

This guy is a loser who did this to create publicity for himself and because he needs his money back. He doesn't like Tony Bennett. He wanted Madonna. Can you believe it?

USA Today
DECEMBER 14, 1995

I've always been a good chipper and putter. I have great feel. I don't know why. I can feel the putt when I stand over it. I kill guys with my putting.

Golf Magazine
NOVEMBER 1993

On building golf courses:

I think being Trump is a huge asset and it's a huge liability. I think that if I were a developer up in Westchester, I think probably [the golf course plan] would have been a little less controversial, probably a lot less controversial. But it wouldn't have been the quality that it is.

New York Observer
APRIL 5, 1999

On Himself

People either love me or they hate me.

Miami Herald
MARCH 24, 1995

My life is an open book. I am a good son. I am a good parent. I've got four wonderful kids. I've been married twice. I don't smoke. I've never had a glass of alcohol. I've never taken illegal drugs of any kind. I've never even had a cup of coffee.

Advocate
FEBRUARY 15, 2000

I think I'm passionate about life. I'm
passionate about everything I do.

> *USA Today*
> MARCH 1, 2000

I've never had a drink in my life
because of the fact that I had a
brother that had a problem with
alcohol.

> *Larry King Live*
> OCTOBER 8, 1999

I only have winners, whether it's
[The Apprentice] or real estate in
New York.

> *Philadelphia Inquirer*
> APRIL 5, 2004

On his hair:

It's been good to me over the years.
Maybe that's my problem.

San Jose Mercury News
JANUARY 28, 2004

More about hair:

The reason my hair looks so neat all
the time is because I don't have to
deal with the elements very often.
I live in the building where I work.
I take an elevator from my bedroom
to my office. The rest of the time,
I'm either in my stretch limousine,
my private jet, my helicopter, or my
private club in Palm Beach, Florida.

USA Today
APRIL 5, 2004

Still more:

I actually had somebody come up to
me who was interviewing me and
said, "Well, what about the hair?"
And then she just got off the chair
and she just pulled my hair up.
And she said, "It's real," and "I don't
believe it." So, anyway, in the end, I
don't know if anything matters. You
feel comfortable and you just do it.

The Oprah Winfrey Show
APRIL 8, 2004

On being a celebrity:

I like it, but I would be happy if it
weren't 100 percent of the time.

Chicago Tribune
APRIL 2, 2004

*What he learned about himself during
the financial turnaround in the 1990s:*

A lot of friends of mine went
bankrupt, which I never did, and
you never heard from them again—
they're gone. I fought back, and
now my company is many times
bigger than it was in the early '90s
or '80s. I guess I just learned that
I could handle pressure, and some
people just can't. I mean, I owed
$9.2 billion and I was in deep
trouble, and friends of mine who
weren't in nearly as much trouble
as I was failed.

Los Angeles Daily News
MARCH 29, 2004

All the networks wanted to do a
reality show with me. They wanted
to follow me down the hallway with
a camera and into meetings. But I
am by far the largest developer in
the city now, and you can't get any
business done that way.

San Francisco Chronicle
MARCH 28, 2004

I get more abuse on the hair. It's
been this way since the time I was
in high school. . . . I don't like to
change things. It seems to me to be
working. Is it that bad?

Philadelphia Inquirer
MARCH 20, 2004

It's so much celebrity, I can't even walk outside. It used to be that it was hard to walk outside, now it's impossible.

> *Philadelphia Inquirer*
> MARCH 20, 2004

No, it's never been my nature [to be shy]. I think when you're born, you are a certain way and I think you don't change.

> *Philadelphia Inquirer*
> MARCH 20, 2004

I want it mahogany, I like mahogany, the rich look.

> *Monterey County (California) Herald*
> MARCH 12, 2004

On giving a tour of a penthouse
apartment in one of his properties:

This is called luxury, this is Trump
luxury. One of the most luxurious
buildings in the world. . . . You see
why Trump is Trump.

> *Associated Press*
> APRIL 13, 2004

I was a great genius in the '80s.
Then I was a great moron in the
early '90s. That's probably why
I bought this pageant—so I could
get a date. Now they call me a
genius again. It's great.

> *Associated Press*
> FEBRUARY 7, 1999

*While in the Caribbean for the Miss
Universe pageant, Trump said he was
interested in investing there:*

You go to some places and you have
a good feeling and you go to other
places and you don't have a good
feeling. I'm very much an instinct
person—I go by my gut. I just have
a very good feeling about Trinidad
and Tobago, and that's because of
the people.

> *Associated Press*
> MAY 26, 1999

*Trump insists that he is a hands-on
manager who runs his own show:*

Nobody owns me.

> *New York Post*
> APRIL 18, 1999

*Trump ran into neighborhood opposition
when erecting Trump World Tower across
from the United Nations building in
New York City:*

If someone else was building it, there
would be no opposition. I build the
highest-end buildings in New York.
They sell for the most per square foot
of anybody. That makes me happy,
but because of the high profile, I
tend to bring out the worst in people.

> *Miami Herald*
> FEBRUARY 7, 1999

What I do is successful because of
the aesthetics. People love my
buildings and my pageants.

> *New York Times*
> JANUARY 10, 1999

All day long it's helicopters. It's nuts.

Palm Beach Post
JANUARY 5, 2000

It's not bad to sell things. I owned them, and I sold them. That's why the banks like me. They love my reputation.

New York Times
MARCH 28, 2004

Upon hearing that HBO was developing a film based on Trump's battle with Steve Wynn in Atlantic City:

I want to be played by a very handsome, very brilliant person.

New York Post
DECEMBER 6, 2003

I don't like talking about failure.
I don't even like thinking about
failure. You know, when people tell
me there's this new food that causes
cancer, I say, "Do me a favor: Don't
even mention that word." I don't
want to hear about any of that stuff.

Milwaukee Journal Sentinel
NOVEMBER 25, 2003

If I trip going out of my apartment,
it ends up being a front-page story.

Palm Beach Post
APRIL 15, 2004

I'm not the type of guy who gives
second chances.

During *The Apprentice,*
cited by the *Chicago Tribune*
MARCH 11, 2004

I can't help it that I'm a celebrity.
What am I going to do, hide under
a stone?

> *USA Today*
> FEBRUARY 27, 2004

Generally when I become more
involved in a company . . . they
tend to work.

> *Reno (Nevada) Gazette-Journal*
> FEBRUARY 5, 2004

On his employees:

I don't care what they think because
I'm the boss. If they don't like it,
tough [darts].

> *Aberdeen American News*
> JANUARY 19, 2004

I've probably been in more political
fights than anyone my age.

Hartford Courant
JUNE 3, 1994

The fact is, I am always eager to take
an active part in charities in the areas
in which I have homes or businesses.
I feel that is a responsibility I should
not shirk.

Miami Herald
DECEMBER 11, 2001

I've worked very hard. I've focused
more in the past ten years than I have
since I started the business. I loved
coming back from adversity.

Hoya (Georgetown University)
DECEMBER 4, 2001

I'm not a big fan of the handshake.
I think it's barbaric. I mean, they
have medical reports all the time.
Shaking hands, you catch colds, you
catch the flu, you catch this. You
catch all sorts of things. Who knows
what you don't catch?

Later Today
OCTOBER 6, 1999

Clinton was shaking hands with 500
or 600 people, he then got into the
back of the presidential limo, grabs
a sandwich and he eat its, and no
problem. I wish I could be like that.
I just can't.

Rivera Live
NOVEMBER 26, 1999

I have no regrets. I really have none.
I have had an incredible life, I have
learned a lot. I probably learned
more during my downtime, during
my bad time, financially, than I ever
learned before.

Larry King Live
JULY 23, 1997

I'm always looking for more
excitement in life. I look at life as
one time—here we are, it's a one-
time go-around. I'm always looking
for more excitement.

Saturday Night With Connie Chung
FEBRUARY 24, 1990

Trump was asked to host Saturday Night Live, *which competed in the same time slot as Howard Stern's TV show. Trump said he would consider the offer but had to check with Stern first:*

I don't want to mess up Howard's ratings.

Chicago Tribune
AUGUST 20, 1998

This country is essentially in huge debt. And who understands debt better than I?

Saturday Today
OCTOBER 9, 1999

Normally I only eat steak.

Financial Times
JUNE 15, 1996

I think that there are temptations
and obstacles and things that I have
that other people don't have that
really make life very difficult, in
terms of heaven, in terms of going
to that incredible place, which
I believe exists. So I try and be as
good as possible.

Dateline NBC
OCTOBER 31, 1997

Everybody wants to shoot at me
because it's me.

Chicago Tribune
OCTOBER 27, 1996

I see myself as a very honest guy
stationed in a very corrupt world.

> *Washington Times*
> APRIL 18, 1995

I've gone from the highest plateau
to the point where the world was
beating me up. Some individuals
who could have helped me didn't
try. I will try to get even with them.

> *Times* (London)
> JUNE 19, 1996

I've always wanted a boat bigger
than the queen's.

> *Philadelphia Inquirer*
> JUNE 14, 1996

I like to go first class. It's the only
way I do business.

> *Crain's Chicago Business*
> APRIL 22, 1996

Vision is my best asset. I know what
sells and I know what people want.

> *Playboy*
> MARCH 1990

I think my truthfulness sometimes
gets a little bit blunt and that does
put people off.

> CNN's *People In the News*
> APRIL 3, 2004

I think that the name has been a
great asset, but I would also say this:
Nobody has gotten more bad publicity
over the years than Donald Trump.

> *Capital Report*
> APRIL 1, 2004

You'll never see me sitting in the
corner sucking my thumb. The name
Trump will be hotter than ever.

> *Business Week*
> MARCH 23, 1992

At thirty-seven, no one has done
more than I in the last seven years.

> *New York Times*
> AUGUST 7, 1983

I don't kid myself. . . . It's not because I'm such a great guy [that I get invited to parties]. The reason is that people who run charities know that I've got wealthy friends and can get them to buy tables.

Toronto Star
DECEMBER 26, 1987

It was easier for me ten years ago. Nobody knew who I was and nobody cared. Then, I wasn't the guy everyone was trying to stop.

Los Angeles Times
APRIL 7, 1985

Pressure doesn't upset my sleep.
I like throwing balls into the air—
and I dream like a baby.

Playboy
MARCH 1990

I tend to thrive on solving problems,
on doing what's not supposed to be
able to be done. And I'm not sure
that's 100 percent typical or normal.
In fact, I'm sure it's not at all typical,
but it's something I do, and I actually
like what I do so much that I find it
hard to go on vacation. I find what
other people call relaxation does not
feel very relaxing at all.

Life
JANUARY 1989

I can sit down with the most sophisticated people in the arts in New York and get along fabulously with them. If I want to, I can convince them that I know as much about something as they do, and I don't.

> *Time*
> JANUARY 16, 1989

Trump has a bulletproof sauna and a lead-lined towel closet with a false rear wall for quick escapes:

That's for when they come in with the machine guns.

> *Life*
> JANUARY 1989

On Life

All men are not created equal. Some are born with a genius and some are born without. Now, you need that. If you don't have that, you can forget it.

CNN's *Late Edition with Wolf Blitzer*
MARCH 21, 2004

[Contestants on *The Apprentice*] arrive in a limo at Trump Tower, and when they're fired, they leave in a cab. That's how life is.

San Francisco Chronicle
MARCH 28, 2004

Be paranoid. Now that sounds
terrible, but you have to realize that
people, sadly, sadly, are very vicious.
You think we're so different from
the lions in the jungle?

> *Kansas City Star*
> FEBRUARY 11, 2000

If someone screws you, screw them
back harder.

> *USA Today*
> JANUARY 17, 2000

You want to lead a relatively normal
life, if that's possible for guys like me.
Life's a vicious place. No different
than a jungle.

> *USA Today*
> MARCH 12, 2004

You know, there's always gonna be nepotism, whether it's a friendship or whether it's children, nepotism . . . that's the way the world works.

New York Post, citing *20/20*
with Barbara Walters
FEBRUARY 6, 2004

You're not going to go into a very safe little place and just lock the door and never come out. I just don't think you can do that. And I am a fatalist. I say hey, what happens, happens, and maybe it's predestined, who knows?

Larry King Live
JULY 23, 1997

Everything in life to me is a
psychological game, a series of
challenges you either meet or don't.
I am always testing people who
work for me.

Playboy
MARCH 1990

Things that are great always seem to
work out.

New York Daily News
MAY 30, 1998

I like to look at things as having no
limit, but there was always a limit.
I found that out in life. There was
always a limit.

Dateline NBC
OCTOBER 31, 1997

On turning fifty:

It's got a lot of positives. You've got the experience factor now, and you also have the good health and strength. It's a powerful age.

New York Times
JUNE 14, 1996

I think when you come out of the womb you're a certain personality. You can change somewhat, but essentially you're always going to be that way.

Miami Herald
MARCH 24, 1995

You know what? Life is full of risks.

USA Today
FEBRUARY 27, 2004

You can't give up. You are going to have times when you feel there's no light at the end of the tunnel. I had times like that and I had a choice: I could sit in the corner with my thumb in my mouth, or I could fight. My advice to you is: Punch like hell and don't take no for an answer.

St. Petersburg Times
MAY 7, 1996

The point is that things can turn around, and they can turn around very rapidly.

Remarks to the Cuban-American
National Foundation in Miami, Florida
NOVEMBER 15, 1999

We have to be doing this for some reason. There has to be a reason. And I believe that there is in fact a reason, and I believe heaven could be that reason.

Good Morning America
DECEMBER 2, 1999

I had some great teachers at the Wharton School and at other places. And, boy, when you get a great teacher, and you have the right class and you can get the kind of attention, it makes all the difference in the world.

Hardball with Chris Matthews
NOVEMBER 19, 1999

We're here for a short time. When we're gone, most people don't care, and in some cases they're quite happy about it.

Time
JANUARY 16, 1989

Most people that drink, I've found, have a problem with it. I had a friend who I respected, but who would get totally bombed, and I'd be carrying him out by his arms and legs.

New York Post
JANUARY 29, 2004

On the Media

Well, I think some of the press are
extremely talented and honorable
and honest people. I think some of
the press is total scum.

CNN's *Late Edition with Wolf Blitzer*
NOVEMBER 28, 1999

I mean, until—as I told you before,
if I come up with a cure to cancer,
if I don't get ratings, I'm not going
to be on your show. We know that.
All right?

Rivera Live
NOVEMBER 26, 1999

They've had me out with people
that I've never even heard of before,
I've never seen. I've been dating
some of the most incredible women
in the world, according to them,
and I'm trying to figure out where
are these people? Where are they?

The Geraldo Rivera Show
MAY 16, 1997

The fact is that I don't like publicity. I
absolutely hate doing interviews. . . .
By the way, not this interview. This
is much nicer. I'm enjoying this.
You understand.

People
DECEMBER 7, 1987

Nobody has had worse things
written about them than me.

Playboy
MAY 1997

Doonesbury *cartoonist Garry Trudeau*
has skewered Trump for trying to have
people evicted in Atlantic City so he could
expand Trump Plaza casino. Says Trump:

It's a low blow. He's a third-rate
talent. And it's too bad that he's
allowed to write this garbage. The
good news is he's been covering me
for years and it seems very few
people read what he writes.

Commercial Appeal
(Memphis, Tennessee)
FEBRUARY 21, 1997

You can have the greatest public relations firm in the world, [but] if you're not a certain type the papers aren't going to buy it. What I have done is build the most beautiful buildings in the best locations, and I'm thirty-eight, and I like to live in a certain way. That whole combination leads up to something.

> *Washington Post*
> NOVEMBER 15, 1984

There are a lot of interesting things happening. I think you will do the comeback of the decade story.

> *Newsday*
> APRIL 21, 1991

I don't believe in cheating. But if
I look at somebody or somebody
looks at me, immediately they do
Don Juan stories.

Time
FEBRUARY 26, 1990

I've been asked the same questions
a million times now, and I don't
particularly like talking about my
personal life. Nonetheless, I understand that getting press can be very
helpful in making deals.

Life
JANUARY 1989

On Money

It's pretty irrelevant whether I'm worth $2 billion or $5 billion.

New York Post
JANUARY 20, 2000

Trump says that in 1993 he and his then-wife Marla Maples saw a beggar on the street. At the time, Trump had a negative net worth, owing debts of about $900 million:

I said, "Do you know that right now that man is worth $900 million more than I am?"

Saint Paul Pioneer Press
JANUARY 8, 2000

[Money] is a scorecard. It's fun. But I don't do things to make money. I do it because I love it, and I happen to make money with it. But I do it because I love it.

Dateline NBC
APRIL 17, 2004

Rich people are great survivors, and, by nature fall into two categories—those who have inherited and those who've made it. Those who have made it and chosen not to do anything are generally very timid, afraid of losing what they've got, and who can blame them? Others are great risk takers and produce a hell of a lot more or go bust.

Playboy
MARCH 1990

The payback [of giving to charity] is in your mind. Giving just gives you a good feeling, because you've been generous.

USA Today
FEBRUARY 13, 2004

I love real estate. I love hard assets. There's something about paper that I don't like, you know. You buy stock and you say—have a little piece of paper. And "Gee, is that where my $10,000 or my $20 million went?"

The Oprah Winfrey Show
APRIL 8, 2004

While I was the icon of good times, I was also the icon of bad times.

Miami Herald
MARCH 24, 1995

Money makes life easier, but it
doesn't make you happy.

> *Playboy*
> MAY 1997

I just don't want to [give to charity]
now. I want to do it maybe at an
older age. Or death.

> *New Orleans Times-Picayune*
> OCTOBER 31, 1997

When it comes to [paying top dollar
for] pilots, doctors, accountants, I
don't chisel.

> *Time*
> JANUARY 16, 1989

On Politics

Hundreds and hundreds of young
people killed [in the war in Iraq].
And what about the people coming
back with no arms and no legs? Not
to mention the other side. All those
Iraqi kids who've been blown to
pieces. And it turns out that all the
reasons for the war were blatantly
wrong. All this for nothing!

Esquire
AUGUST 2004

I'm too forthright. I'm too—I think
I'm too honest. But I do believe I'm
too forthright to be a politician.

Evans & Novak
DECEMBER 27, 1997

I can be very politically correct. I went
to the Wharton School of Finance.
I got very good marks. I know what
to say if I have to say it. Sometimes
I choose not to do that. Sometimes
I choose to say something just to
get a result.

CEO Wire
JULY 19, 2004

I have made the tough decisions,
always with an eye toward the
bottom line. Perhaps it's time
America was run like a business.

Advocate
FEBRUARY 15, 2000

I had enormous fun thinking about a presidential candidacy and count it as one of my great life experiences. Although I must admit that it still doesn't compare with completing one of the great skyscrapers of Manhattan, I cannot rule out another bid for the presidency in 2004.

"What I Saw at the Revolution,"
by Donald J. Trump, *New York Times*
FEBRUARY 19, 2000

I think the only difference between me and the other candidates is that I'm more honest and my women are more beautiful.

Morning Call
(Allentown, Pennsylvania)
NOVEMBER 21, 1999

We have no choice but to assume
that had Buchanan been president,
he would have allowed Hitler to wage
uncontested war on defenseless
civilian populations. We must also
assume that Buchanan would have
conducted his policy with the belief
that Hitler had no ill will toward the
United States. He would have been
our version of Neville Chamberlain.

> "Buchanan Is Too Wrong to
> Correct" by Donald J. Trump,
> *Los Angeles Times*
> OCTOBER 31, 1999

In good times, you don't get reform
parties to do very well. . . . The
Reform Party can only really jell
if times are bad.

> *Today*
> FEBRUARY 15, 2000

For those who suggest that this [presidential bid] has just been a promotion, I want to strongly deny that.

New York Post
FEBRUARY 15, 2000

The Reform Party now includes a Klansman, Mr. Duke, a neo-Nazi, Mr. Buchanan, and a communist, Ms. Fulani. This is not company I wish to keep.

Contra Costa Times
(Walnut Creek, California),
citing a prepared statement
FEBRUARY 14, 2000

I'm tired of politicians being president, because I see the lousy job they do, and I'm just tired of it. And I think a lot of other people are.

Larry King Live
OCTOBER 8, 1999

Since the beginning of my political exploratory effort, I have consistently said that I was only interested in running if I had the prospect of winning. . . . Without Jesse, the Reform Party is just an extremist shell and cannot be a force or even a factor in 2000.

New York Daily News,
citing a statement
FEBRUARY 14, 2000

Historically, I've worked with politicians and gotten along with politicians. I get along with all sides.

Courier-Post
(Cherry Hill, New Jersey)
JANUARY 29, 2000

While he was mulling over whether to run for president:

I'm not prepared to throw [my money] away. I'd rather go to Atlantic City and take a bet on the tables, because, to be honest with you, unless there's total unity in this party, it would be foolhardy to run.

Hill (Washington, D.C.)
JANUARY 26, 2000

I'd really like to make the race,
particularly, if the nominees are
"Gush" and "Bore."

> *Commercial Appeal*
> (Memphis, Tennessee)
> JANUARY 21, 2000

Ours is the only presidential
campaign that makes money.

> *USA Today*
> JANUARY 17, 2000

On President Bush:

So far, I've been very, very saddened
by the fact that he certainly doesn't
seem like Albert Einstein.

> *Hotline,* citing *60 Minutes II*
> JANUARY 12, 2000

There's a big difference between creating wealth and being a member of the lucky sperm club.

Inside Politics
JANUARY 7, 2000

For years, I watched politicians brag how poor they were, how poor their family is, how poor their grandparents were, and how their families have been losers for years and years. And, "Elect me, because I'm a loser."

Contra Costa Times
(Walnut Creek, California)
JANUARY 9, 2000

On President Clinton:

I really think that Ken Starr was terrible. But I think the president handled it terribly. And it's a shame, because he could have gone down as a very good and even great president. It's a shame.

> *Today*
> OCTOBER 8, 1999

I feel it's an important thing to contribute [to candidates] even if in not all instances the people agree exactly with me. But I do contribute a lot.

> *Evans & Novak*
> DECEMBER 27, 1997

We have people negotiating trade
that maybe never negotiated before.
And if you look at other countries,
they have their smartest, their
toughest, their best negotiators, and
we're not going to beat them unless
we get ours.

> *This Week*
> DECEMBER 5, 1999

But certainly, if I were president,
women would play a major role in
the administration.

> *Good Morning America*
> DECEMBER 2, 1999

Trump proposed a 14.25 percent tax on net worth of the wealthy, which would raise about $6 billion and wipe out the national debt immediately:

The plan I am proposing today does not involve smoke and mirrors, phony numbers, financial gimmicks, or the usual economic chicanery you usually find in Disneyland-on-the-Potomac.

CNN.com
NOVEMBER 9, 1999

I think [Ross Perot's] going to have a helluva chance of getting elected because frankly, I'm not sure that there is an alternative.

Real Estate Weekly
MAY 20, 1992

People don't want to be taken
advantage of. They know this country
will not be taken advantage of for
one minute if I were involved.

> *Toronto Star*
> DECEMBER 26, 1987

There's nothing wrong with America's
foreign defense policy that a little
backbone can't cure.

> *Guardian* (Manchester)
> SEPTEMBER 4, 1987

The Russians are not the ones to fear.
It's Third World oil countries that
will have the [nuclear] technology
soon. Then the world will be a very
hot place.

> *Business Week*
> JULY 20, 1987

On Fidel Castro:

He's a murderer, he's a killer, he's a bad guy in every respect, and, frankly, the embargo against Cuba must stand if for no other reason than, if it does stand, he will come down.

> Remarks to the Cuban-
> American National Foundation
> in Miami, Florida
> NOVEMBER 15, 1999

Well, I'm very liberal, quite liberal, when it comes to social and health issues. And I believe that I'm quite conservative—I wouldn't say Jesse Helms conservative, but I'm quite conservative when it . . . comes to the military and our defense and our enemies.

> *Rivera Live*
> NOVEMBER 26, 1999

On Real Estate

I'm the greatest developer in New York, and I plan to keep going.

New York Post
AUGUST 4, 2000

And, you know, I just, I love real estate. It's tangible, it's solid, it's beautiful. It's artistic, from my standpoint, and I just love real estate.

Wall $treet Week with Fortune
JULY 26, 2002

In my business, in the real estate business, guys are very old. Guys go into their eighties and nineties, and they're still doing deals. In a lot of businesses, they sort of retire when they're sixty-five or seventy, and they retire. So, I think I want to go as long as I can go.

CNN's *Late Edition with Wolf Blitzer*
MARCH 21, 2004

I put my name on buildings because it sells better. I don't do it because I need that [for my ego].

Larry King Live
OCTOBER 8, 1999

[The entertainment business is] as mean as real estate. Real estate can be very cruel. I would say the executives in Hollywood are every bit as vicious as the executives in New York real estate.

Philadelphia Inquirer
MARCH 20, 2004

I build buildings, I'm the best at it. But I do this for fun. I'm getting $100,000 an episode [for *The Apprentice*]. You think that if I get an extra couple of bucks from doing a television show, that means something? It doesn't.

Copley News Service
APRIL 25, 2004

Nobody gets prices [rents] like I
get prices.

> *New York Post*
> APRIL 18, 1999

Honestly, I'm having fun, and it's
great to be a big TV star, but what I
really like doing is building buildings.

> *Palm Beach Post*
> APRIL 15, 2004

*On opponents to a residential skyscraper
Trump was planning to build near the
United Nations:*

It's clear on the face that the few
opponents, and they are few, aren't
even able to read the simplest of
English.

> Associated Press
> APRIL 23, 1999

*While scouting a location to build
a race-car speedway:*

It's going to be a big day for
either New York, New Jersey,
or Connecticut.

> *Austin American-Statesman*
> MARCH 13, 1999

If you own a great piece of land in
the middle of New York City, guess
what? No one can copy it.

> BPI Entertainment News Wire
> NOVEMBER 20, 2003

Nobody loved the World Trade
Center until its death. . . . Now that
it's gone, everybody loves it.

> *New York Post*
> SEPTEMBER 13, 2003

We all want the World Trade Center to be built again—exactly as it was, maybe higher. But in the real world, nobody's going to go in there. Who's going to go on the floor where Cantor Fitzgerald was?

Palm Beach Post
NOVEMBER 17, 2001

I like tall, skinny buildings. That's what my public likes.

United Press International
JULY 18, 2001

What can I say? The [Trump] name creates value.

Newsday
OCTOBER 30, 1998

I've always thought that New York should have the tallest building in the world.

New York Times
OCTOBER 16, 1998

I prefer one great building to two less-than-great buildings.

Miami Herald
JANUARY 24, 1995

While considering the sale of Trump's Castle Casino Resort in Atlantic City to the Hard Rock Cafe:

If they pay enough money, I would allow them to put their name on it. They're buying into the building.

Times Union
(Albany, New York)
OCTOBER 4, 1996

In England your past architecture
is some of the greatest in the world.
You have got great country homes
and great estates and town houses
but you have not captured the idea
of glamour.

Financial Times
JUNE 15, 1996

I was going to be a movie producer.
In fact, I applied, at one point, I
remember, to the USC School of
Cinema. But then decided that the
movie business wasn't as good as
the real estate business.

CNN's *People in the News*
APRIL 3, 2004

[The World Trade Center] represented freedom, it represented power and majesty, and it really became a target. One of the things that I feel we have to do is build our buildings stronger so that they can withstand attack if necessary.

20/20
OCTOBER 3, 2001

[My father] was a wonderful negotiator. He was able to build for less money than the guy across the street, faster than the people across the street, and have a better product in the end. And he taught me that.

Market Week with Maria Bartiromo
JULY 6, 2001

The reason I'm doing so well—it's not because of me, I can tell you that. The reason I'm doing so well at City Planning, etc., is the city needs jobs.

> *Real Estate Weekly*
> DECEMBER 23, 1992

In other cities, if you are a developer, they erect you a statue. . . . In New York, if you are a developer, you've got a problem.

> *Real Estate Weekly*
> MAY 26, 1993

I have the best diamonds in the city of New York as far as location.

> *New York Times*
> AUGUST 7, 1983

I play to people's fantasies. . . . The more unattainable the apartments seemed, the more people wanted them.

Toronto Star
DECEMBER 26, 1987

I've taken a very good business, real estate, and I've added a tremendous element of excitement to it. I've added quality to it. I've added showmanship.

People
DECEMBER 7, 1987

What I have done is build the most beautiful buildings in the best locations.

Forbes
OCTOBER 28, 1985

I don't know [about future projects].
With a fertile, creative mind,
hopefully there will be lots of
things to do.

Business Week
JULY 22, 1985

*In 1974, Trump optioned an abandoned
rail yard from the bankrupt Penn Central
Railroad. He promoted it as the site for
New York City's new convention center:*

The convention center was a victory
against the establishment that nobody
thought I was going to win.

Los Angeles Times
APRIL 7, 1985

Trump bought gold in 1971 and sold it in 1982 for a reported $73 million profit:

It was a good investment. A lot easier than building buildings, I'll tell you that.

> *Washington Post*
> NOVEMBER 15, 1984

On purchasing the Commodore Hotel even though the nearby Chrysler Building was in foreclosure:

I saw all those people coming out of Grand Central Terminal, and I said to myself, "How bad can this be?"

> *New York Times*
> APRIL 8, 1984

On his penthouse in Trump Tower:

If this were on the ceiling of the
Sistine Chapel, it would be very
much in place in terms of quality.
This is really what you call talent,
more talent than the schmucks
who go around throwing paint
on the canvas.

> *Time*
> JANUARY 16, 1989

*Trump is often the subject of lawsuits
because of his ambitious real estate
plans:*

They always sue when you get
zoning of any substantial size.
The lawsuits are not meaningful.

> *Real Estate Weekly*
> APRIL 28, 1993

I like going against the tide. Oftentimes, being a contrarian, oftentimes that will work. That worked out on Wall Street. I bought buildings on Wall Street when everybody was selling, and now those buildings are very valuable.

Today
NOVEMBER 3, 1997

On his thirty-ninth birthday Trump bought Hilton Hotels Corporation's Atlantic City casino for $320 million:

I got the castle for my birthday.

Business Week
JULY 22, 1985

On Success

I believe in success.

Contra Costa Times
(Walnut Creek, California)
JANUARY 9, 2000

They're saying, "Let's fight Trump because it's Trump." They think it's glamorous. It gives them something to do.

Chicago Tribune
OCTOBER 27, 1996

Every successful person has a very large ego.

Playboy
MARCH 1990

Failure to me is just not being on top, it's just not being there. And you know, it's something that I don't exactly cherish.

Good Morning America
DECEMBER 2, 1999

The success I'm having now is more satisfying because I have more respect for success. Before, it was like everything just happened. I never missed. Now I realize it's not that easy.

Playboy
MAY 1997

I have an unlimited appetite for pain. That's a secret to my success. I just can't give up.

New York Times
JUNE 10, 2001

My father was successful, but it was
a different kind of success. I didn't
grow up like this. When I played golf
I played at the public course. I'd go
to the state park and wait four hours
to tee off when I was fourteen.

Washington Post
NOVEMBER 15, 1984

If there's a concrete wall in front of
you, you have to go through that
wall. You can't give up. And you have
to love what you're doing or you'll
never be good at it.

Dateline NBC, citing
The Apprentice
APRIL 17, 2004

On the Women in His Life

The fact is, there are certain women who are able to use sex appeal to win. Because I'm such a diplomat, I want to say to never use it. But the fact is, life is loaded with it.

The Oprah Winfrey Show
APRIL 8, 2004

Trump was asked if he liked East Coast or West Coast girls better:

I like 'em all. Even the ones in the middle, too. I like 'em all.

During a reception in the Kiel Center, St. Louis, reported in the *Contra Costa Times* (Walnut Creek, California) FEBRUARY 13, 2000

Usually, I build buildings. I have to
deal with the unions, the Mob, some
of the roughest men you've ever
seen in your life. I come here [to
the Miss USA Pageant] and see these
incredible beauties. It's a lot of fun.

Associated Press
FEBRUARY 7, 1999

*On spending his time at fashion shows
in Europe:*

I love looking at the models. . . .
Isn't that disgusting? The women
here are going to walk out saying,
"Isn't that guy a terrible, terrible
barbarian?"

Palm Beach Post
NOVEMBER 26, 2001

They say the weaker sex. Believe me,
that's a misnomer.

The Geraldo Rivera Show
FEBRUARY 6, 1998

On prenuptial agreements:

It's a terrible document. It's ugly,
it's—it's horrible in almost every
way, but you need it. It's very tough
to walk up to a woman or a man
and say, "Listen, darling, I love you
very much, but just in case we get
divorced, this is what you're gonna
be getting, if it's OK with you."

This Morning
JANUARY 9, 1998

About Marla Maples:

I'm not sure I'm as good of a husband as I am a father, but—but I think she has a legitimate complaint in that—in that way. I am not able to spend very much time.

> *Today*
> NOVEMBER 4, 1997

This is a real beauty contest. Others, such as Miss America, are not really beauty contests because they judge a great deal on talent. Miss Universe is all about beauty.

> *New York Daily News*
> MAY 12, 1998

I adore Marla as I do Ivana, but I am just not cut out for marriage. My focus is on my business, and it's never done better.

Larry King's People
in a column in *USA Today*
JULY 28, 1997

Miss Universe has the best-looking girls in the world. They're much better-looking than the Miss America contestants.

New York Daily News
OCTOBER 24, 1996

On his settlement with Ivana:

This money was given to you for
your protection and so that it may
someday go to the children. I sure
as hell did not give it to you so that
it goes to your next husband—
whomever that may be.

> *Austin American-Statesman*
> JULY 22, 1995

I create stars. . . . I have really given
a lot of women great opportunity.
Unfortunately, after they are a star,
the fun is over for me.

> *San Jose Mercury News,*
> citing *PrimeTime Live*
> MARCH 11, 1994

After divorcing Marla Maples, Trump began going out again:

This is one of the worst times in the history of the world to be dating.

San Francisco Chronicle
JULY 8, 1999

I have found in many cases [women] are more effective than a man would be. They're very dedicated to showing me that they can do it.

Washington Post
SEPTEMBER 23, 1989

What Others
Say About Trump

Donald goes absolutely ballistic,
screaming, yelling, cursing, and you
could not print the words he says.
You wouldn't want to be there.

> George Ross, one of Trump's two
> advisers on *The Apprentice,* speaking
> about what happens to disloyal or
> dishonest employees, *Centre Daily
> Times* (State College, Pennsylvania)
> MARCH 30, 2004

Every person who walks into the
store now says, "Oh you're copying
Donald Trump," And I say, "No, he's
copying me."

> Susan Brenner, whose pottery store has
> been named "You're Fired" for more
> than seven years, *Chicago Tribune*
> MARCH 30, 2004

I felt very comfortable that Trump would work. He required zero coaching.

> Mark Burnett, creator of *The Apprentice, Television Week*
> MARCH 29, 2004

He's very, very sharp, which has been proven by his success. Of course, I don't think Trump would be a good example of a Fortune 500 CEO.

> Stephen Standifird, professor of management at the University of San Diego, Copley News Service
> MARCH 28, 2004

The hair, always the hair:

It's the Trumpadour.

> Peter Phe, South Pasadena Internet entrepreneur, *Los Angeles Times*
> MARCH 15, 2004

On Trump calling himself the "biggest real estate developer in New York":

He's a dear friend of mine, but it wouldn't be accurate for him to say that.

> Richard S. LeFrak, head of the real estate family that owns the most residential units in New York City, *New York Times*
> MARCH 28, 2004

I'd comb it back. . . . And I tell you what, I'd love to do it for him [because] everyone will know who did it. . . . There isn't a person on this continent that isn't aware of Trump's hair.

> Sexy Hair Concepts stylist Michael O'Rourke, *Kansas City Star*
> FEBRUARY 25, 2004

Trump is the Madonna of the business world.

> Kerry McCloskey, top fifty finalist
> in last year's competition for
> *The Apprentice, New York Post*
> MARCH 19, 2004

It's never dull. You have to be prepared for anything, you have to be tough.

> Rhona Graff-Riccio,
> Trump's executive assistant,
> Copley News Service
> APRIL 25, 2004

I had a cesarean section with my first child, Connor, and he was the first person who telephoned to see how I was.

> Carolyn Kepcher, Trump's
> second adviser on *The Apprentice,*
> *Washington Post*
> APRIL 18, 2004

When I bring up in seminars or meetings I worked for Trump, I get twenty minutes of "What was he like?" I could have worked for IBM and nobody would say boo. You say you worked for Donald Trump and the amount of intrigue, the amount of curiosity, it's like being around a rock star.

Billy Procida, former Trump
vice president, *Orlando Sentinel*
APRIL 7, 2004

We saw no evidence that he was a serious candidate at all. All this was . . . a serious hustle of the media, and I think the media should send him a massive bill on it.

Reform Party head Pat Choate,
New York Times
FEBRUARY 14, 2000

The one thing I'd say about Donald
is he is what he is.

> Motivational speaker Tony
> Robbins, *Kansas City Star*
> FEBRUARY 11, 2000,

Steve Wynn is jealous because
Donald is richer than him, smarter
than him, and better looking.

> Norma Foederer, a Trump vice
> president, *Philadelphia Inquirer*
> APRIL 23, 1999

I never thought I'd be giving Donald
Trump a reference, but so far the
Trump organization has been an
excellent corporate citizen.

> Gary, Indiana, City Hall spokeswoman
> Sandy Cogan, *Kansas City Star*
> JANUARY 26, 1999

This is not about philanthropy.
You're thinking of Ted Turner. This
is Donald Trump.

> Joseph Connor, U.N. chief of budget
> and management, *Washington Times*
> JANUARY 10, 2001

*Trump publicly apologized for ads he
ran degrading Indians seeking a casino
license:*

The damage is already done. Him
with his millions. The apology is too
late as far as we're concerned. Grow
up and act like a man.

> Mohawk Chief Hilda Smoke,
> *Times Union*
> (Jacksonville, Florida)
> DECEMBER 23, 2000

Donald Trump is a force of nature.

> Philip K. Howard, chairman
> of the Municipal Art Society,
> *Washington Post*
> JANUARY 7, 1999

He was probably the highest-paid
casino executive in the business. And
that doesn't even count the perks,
the helicopter rides, and all that.

> Marvin Roffman, an analyst
> with Roffman Miller Associates,
> *New York Post*
> APRIL 4, 2004

Nobody tells Donald Trump what to do.
You suggest and then he'll add to it.

> Golf course designer Jim Fazio,
> *Palm Beach Post*
> APRIL 26, 1998

Our establishment is for the enjoyment of the young female form, Mr. Trump's is engaged in gambling. I'm not sure which is the bigger vice, but I know there is a distinct difference.

> Mukesh Shretta, who was sued by Trump over the name of her establishment Club Taj Mahal, *Atlanta Journal-Constitution* AUGUST 2, 1996

Every morning he wakes up and says, "Who can I sue?"

> PR counselor John Scanlon, *O'Dwyer's PR Services Report* FEBRUARY 1996

Donald Trump became a controversial person and it worked for him.

> Preston Robert Tisch, president of the
> Loews Corporation, *New York Times*
> AUGUST 7, 1983

To work for Donald, you absolutely have to love him, because he will absolutely drive you crazy.

> Blanche Sprague, executive
> vice president of the Trump
> Organization, *Toronto Star*
> DECEMBER 26, 1987

He sues almost everybody. . . . He's either crying that somebody's trying to cheat him, or somebody else is saying that he's trying to cheat them.

> David Rozenholc, attorney for
> tenants of a building Trump wanted
> to tear down, *Business Week*
> JULY 22, 1985

In a way, Donald Trump's best ally
has been the business cycle.

> City Parks Commissioner Henry
> Stern, formerly a city councilman,
> *New York Times*
> APRIL 7, 1985

He has an uncanny sense of knowing
that something is a good deal when
it looks dismal to everyone else.

> Trump's attorney Roy M. Cohn,
> *New York Times*
> APRIL 8, 1984

There is nothing particularly unusual
about Donald Trump except that he
got richer than most and he has an
ugly haircut.

> Professor Edward Hill,
> Cleveland State University
> *Independent* (London)
> JUNE 10, 1990

The rumor of my romantic association with Donald Trump is untrue, unfounded, and outrageous. The reason I'm going public with my outrage over this allegation is that I had hoped that Donald Trump would issue his own statement of the rumor being completely unfounded, and that has not happened quickly enough.

> former Olympic skating champion
> Peggy Fleming, *Los Angeles Times*
> FEBRUARY 15, 1990

The whole Trump style is to put up other people's money and let them take the risk.

> Marvin Roffman, analyst at
> Janney Montgomery Scott,
> *Washington Post*
> MARCH 25, 1990